T0208929

SOLDIER
for
CHRIST

A Calling to Enlist, Train, and Deploy

KEITH PATE

WESTBOW
PRESS®
A DIVISION OF THOMAS NELSON
& ZONDERVAN

WestBow Press books may be ordered through
booksellers or by contacting:

WestBow Press
A Division of Thomas Nelson & Zondervan
1663 Liberty Drive
Bloomington, IN 47403
www.westbowpress.com
1 (866) 928-1240

Author Credits: Wounded Warrior, Bronze
Star recipient, and Stroke Survivor

ISBN: 978-1-9736-9565-3 (sc)
ISBN: 978-1-9736-9564-6 (e)

Print information available on the last page.

WestBow Press rev. date: 07/08/2020

In loving memory of my mother,
Dorinda Watson Pate.

CONTENTS

FOREWORD

I met Keith last summer at Hernando Baptist Church. We had a missions emphasis night and he had come with his neighbor and my friend, Shane. Shane introduced me to Keith, telling me that he played football on the 2000 national championship team at Delta State University. Since I serve as the team chaplain, Shane figured we would both enjoy getting to know each other as we had such a common interest in the Fighting Okra.

We did not have much time that evening to visit and get to know each other, but in that moment, I was intrigued. What was Keith's story? Here was a man in front of me who was chiseled in his muscular strength, had a very clean haircut and style, was dressed like one of the cool kids from school, and was walking with a crutch. His voice was high-pitched and squeaky.

As the sovereignty of God prevailed, I had the chance to visit with Keith about two weeks later. I was returning a tool that I had borrowed from Shane and Keith happened to be at his house. Shane had recently built a new woodworking shop and wanted me to take a minute and enjoy his new place of escape. Shane, Keith, and I found ourselves out in the shop. The tour didn't take long, and my mind was going back to the question "What is the story with Keith?"

It just didn't add up. All I could imagine was a car wreck or something similar had caused this national championship football player to now have to balance himself with that crutch.

As I often do, I just came out and asked Keith, as I reached out and touched the crutch that he was using, "What is this about? What's your story?"

I won't spoil it for you, but in the next few minutes, as he told me all about his crutch, all I could think was getting him in front of my Delta State football players!

I asked if he would come and share with the team sometime. To my delight, he said yes! Then I got intentional. "How about this Saturday?" I asked. He looked shocked. Shane spoke up and said, "Keith, I'll cancel whatever I have planned for this Saturday and take you." I chimed in, "Keith, I'll help you!" I offered to make a PowerPoint presentation and ask him some questions. I have found this helps take the pressure off people when they are not used to public speaking. I ensured him that I would help carry the conversation and not embarrass him. Keith looked with a smile and said, "Let's do it!"

We were so excited. You could sense the Holy Spirit's presence right there among us in that woodshop. It was a powerful moment that has become a powerful movement.

When we walked through the house and out the front door, we were confronted with one of the brightest and most beautiful rainbows God has put in the sky. We all got excited again! I said, "Fellas, I don't want to overspiritualize the moment, but I believe that God is pleased with what is happening and just put that there as a reminder that he is good and his promises are everlasting!" Shane and Keith posed for a picture to mark the moment together. Did I mention that Keith's house is across the street from Shane's house and that the rainbow was positioned perfectly over Keith's house?

Friend, you are about to be challenged and blessed by reading this story. This man named Keith Pate is a dear friend and has become like a brother to me. I'm convinced that he would give me the shirt off his back!

Read and be blessed. When you finish, order another copy and share it with a friend.

Keith, I love you and am so proud to call you my friend and brother in Christ Jesus, our Lord!

Get some Kleenex and read on!

INTRODUCTION

I absolutely hate talking about myself, but I realize the importance of my audience understanding the type of person I was before my injury. Do not take listing my accomplishments as being overconfident or being conceited. It is *very* important to me that you know I'm not seeking any glory or recognition from my story. I don't know why God is using me so much right now, but I'm completely unworthy. I just want to tell people what God has done for me and that he can do it for each of you too. There's no situation in life he can't bring you out of. I hope you see him through my story. I was very accomplished, I was independent, I had many adult responsibilities, I had a great job and many friends, and I was in very good health. I didn't ask anyone for help or prayers. If something was broke, I was going to fix it. I didn't depend on anyone for anything. I was the big, bad athlete and army officer. I walked into the hospital cafeteria in Atlanta and was able to see all the people I thought were much worse than me. I wondered inside what I was doing among all of them. Reality of my situation began to sink in. I could not feed myself or bathe myself anymore. I wasn't the man I used to be, but I realize now that I was on a very long journey to becoming the man God wanted me to be. God broke me down so I have to depend on him for everything, every day. I heard a marine say, "It took a life-changing event for me to appreciate the life I have."

1

SOME GAVE ALL

MSG BILLY RUFF **PFC WILLIAM (BRANDON) DAWSON**

It was 8:00 p.m. on September 24, 2010. I was sitting in an O'Charley's in Olive Brach, Mississippi. I had just ordered my meal. I had just buried a great friend the week before. Things couldn't get any worse, or could they? My phone rang; it was my boss in his less than cheerful voice. He asked me if my dress uniform was ready. I immediately knew he needed me, and it was serious. I kept my uniform cleaned and ready, hanging on a door at home hoping I would never need it. Then he said, "We had a soldier get killed. PFC William Dawson (known as Brandon) from Walls, Mississippi, and I need you to do the notification." As full-time national guard, we were responsible for all military members who resided within the state (active duty or reservist). I gave my drink to the table next to me and hurried to go get dressed.

On the way to his home, I'd received minimum details from our casualty support center that I rehearsed over and over, but they wouldn't come close to preparing me for what I had to do. I would later find out details that haunt me to this day.

I remember walking up to the glass door, heart pounding and knowing I was about to turn upside down the lives of the people I was watching through the door. I had developed a technique in college as a football player for dealing with pressure. I would certainly need it. When I close my eyes, I can still see his face. I had dealt with death many times in my career, but this situation really hit me hard. He had just turned twenty. (He looked so young in the pictures I'd seen.). He had only been in the service one year and was within weeks of returning home from his deployment. Now I had to explain to his mother and younger brother they'd never see him again.

On September 18, 2010, Master Sergeant Billy Ruff, my good military friend, died. He was having a party at his house, and one of his friends was drinking. My friend (being the person he was) volunteered to drive his motorcycle home and wrecked and died as result. He left behind two kids who were still in school. He and I served together for over six years. Billy taught me so much not only about the military but about life also. He was very unselfish. As a platoon sergeant, I often saw him just as dirty as his platoon. He was a worker. When I first met him, he was a supply sergeant. He was alone in a platoon cage getting equipment together, sweating tremendously. I saw him like that many times throughout our careers. We would spend two deployments together, a hurricane, a National Training Center rotation, and years on the full-time staff. He was a staff sergeant when I was hired, and we worked together in several roles in the future. He was a role model. He was someone I looked up to. I can remember him coming to my house and checking on my family while I was away training. I remember us sharing an MRE in the desert of California. I remember us cuddling like boyfriend and girlfriend on a mountain in the same desert (because it was so cold). Now I had to be a pallbearer at his funeral. When I first got the information, my heart sank. It's still hard to believe after so many years. He was a great guy.

These are just a couple of the many stories that remind me of the sacrifices our veterans and their families face. I added these stories during Veterans Day, and then I was asked to keep them because my audience was intrigued by these stories.

- Dec 26, 2010 suffered a near life ending stroke
- Dr's removed 2/3 of my cerebellum
- Given a 10% chance to live
- In 2013 I was told by a Doctor in Jacksonville, FL "I wasn't supposed to walk or sit up"
- I was a 4 year college football player, a college graduate, a master's degree recipient, a 9 yr. military service member, a 2 time war veteran, a modern army combative instructor, a father, a brother, a son. How could this happen

2

INJURY

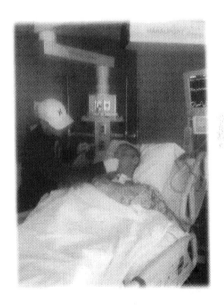

I've been saved since I was about twelve years old; that's just something you do growing up in the south, right? I didn't really begin noticing or fully understanding the impact that God was having on my life until the last four months. I know many people are watching my life, expecting me to fall back into my old ways. I told an acquaintance a couple of weeks ago that once you've hit rock bottom, you *never* want to go back. We all have a story; some are just more visible. I now realize the importance of telling our stories. I've been blessed and have been able to share what God has done for me by speaking with over three thousand people in four months. Wow. I would've never thought.

On January 19, 2019, I was traveling with my friend and neighbor to speak at a wild game dinner at Parkway Baptist Church in Houston, Mississippi. We were listening to a sermon on the radio. The pastor was speaking about how God will use unexpected circumstances in your life to accomplish his will. I am going to tell you how he's used an unexpected circumstance in my life.

When I was thirty-seven years old, it seemed like life was frozen in a bad place. I was going through another very tough time in life. I remember asking God if this was ever going to end. I hadn't been a great person, but I hadn't been what I would consider horrible either. I knew I had a rare story and felt like God had wanted me to tell it for years. I'm very stubborn and imagined my life going in a completely different direction than what God wanted. My stubbornness almost cost me everything. I was forced into bankruptcy; my physical and spiritual life had become nonexistent.

I'm very thankful to my neighbors for being very special friends. For feeding me when I couldn't and for ensuring I walked close to God during these struggles. One evening in late September, my neighbors invited me to eat at their table during a church mission dinner. A Fellowship of Christian Athletes (FCA) staff member who had recently moved here had set up a publicity table during the dinner. The table had a Delta State University (DSU) football helmet on it. I had played forty-five collegiate games wearing a similar helmet, and I had to meet him. I was introduced to Jay Thomason by my neighbor and was immediately intrigued by his bubbly and passionate character. I introduced myself and enjoyed the meal. I assumed that would be the end. I had no idea and couldn't imagine the relationship that would develop between him, the FCA, and me. I still shake my head in awe.

I like to start every event I share at by thanking God; he's the reason I'm able to tell my story. I also like to thank any veterans and their families. As a veteran, there's one word that describes being a veteran, and that is *sacrifice.* When a person has walked away from his family while not knowing if he will see them again, he partially understands the sacrifice. I personally know and understand that sacrifice and am very appreciative of that.

At twenty-nine years of age, I suffered a midline cerebellum infarct (stroke), which is quite rare. I was in a hospital in Tupelo, Mississippi, in the photo above. They had cleaned me up significantly. I went to bed on December 25, 2010, not knowing that when I woke, my life would be forever changed. Early that morning on December 26, 2010, I woke in a daze. My kids were in the bed with me, and my daughter recognized something was wrong and was able to get my brother. He and his wife called an ambulance right away.

I was certainly not prepared for what would come in the following days. While at the North Mississippi Medical Center in Tupelo, I was diagnosed with a hole in my heart that went undetected but doctors were able to repair. The blood clot that formed in my lower extremities was allowed to pass to my cerebellum (brain), causing the stroke. During this time, I was heavily sedated and remember very little. I only know what people have told me. I do know it was a very delicate time and could have gone either way. I was placed in the stroke unit. I had emergency brain surgery to release the pressure that was building and remove three-fourths of my cerebellum that was damaged in the stroke. Doctors also put in some drains.

I had a feeding tube and a breathing tube put in. Once I was stabilized, my dad and I flew to Atlanta, Georgia. It was his first time to fly. I thought I was going to have to give him my bed on the way. I was an inpatient at the Shepherd Center in Atlanta for about three months. I remember rolling into the dining room there for the first time and still believing I shouldn't be there, and the others were much worse than me. I was doing better than I was in Tupelo, but I developed meningitis, which set me back. While there, I was assigned a team of doctors, therapists, and nurses, and we got to work rehabbing.

Things that were once reactive were impossible. The cerebellum is responsible for motor control and coordination; my mind seemed to be doing well, but my body couldn't do things it once could. The removal of my cerebellum greatly impacted my speech, eyesight.

Before I left Atlanta, I had my breathing tube and my feeding tube removed. I also had a central line (an IV that went straight to my heart) removed. I was like a new man.

Afterward, I was transported via ambulance to the Charlie Norwood VA hospital in Augusta, Georgia. I was very angry upon my arrival. I did not know why I had to be moved, and I took my anger out on some of the staff and my family. They wanted to put me in a covered bed to protect me, and I was not having it. Being put in one of those is for someone else, not me. The doctors and staff I worked with were professional and very helpful in my recovery. The next several months were filled with rehab, doctor appointments, and preparing my medical packet for the military board. I was assigned a primary physician, psychiatrist, physician assistant, physical therapist, occupational therapist, speech therapist, vision therapist, recreational therapist, counselor, and nurse case manager.

Two years and one day after my stroke, on December 27, 2012, I was medically retired from the military. By that time, I had been in a wheelchair, then a rolling walker, then two forearm crutches, and now one forearm crutch. I have double vision and a severe speech impediment. I still have a long way to go. I thank God I'm still here though.

Fast-forward to October 2013. I had decided I was going to find the best doctor in the country and he was going to fix me. I had two small kids who depended on me, I had a job/career that I loved, and I had been through so much already. I found a doctor at a clinic in Florida. Imagine my dad and me (two rednecks from Mississippi) loading up in his car and traveling down there. When we arrived, I knew we were in the wrong place. This hospital had valet parking. At thirty-two years old, that doctor sat me down, looked me in the eyes, and said, "Son, I don't know how you're here." For about six months, I lay down. That was really hard to hear. I began to realize he wasn't the best doctor, and he wasn't going to be the one to help me. Maybe God didn't want me fixed. I believe God knew I'd survive, and he wants me to tell my story.

I died twice while in the hospital

3

THE END, MAYBE

My then ten-year-old son likes to say, "My dad died twice in the hospital." I don't say "died" but "coded." I'm kind of torn on whether that's good or bad. It's hard to imagine your ten-year-old son talking about death, but that's also an accomplishment that's pretty hard to match. I got to eat lunch with him at school, and before I went, he gave me strict instructions that if his friends asked me if I died twice, I was to answer, "Yeah." When I graduated Delta State University, I weighed close to 246 pounds, in the military, I dropped to 215 pounds, and then in the hospital, I dropped to 166 pounds. My muscles had grown so weak that I could not swallow. I would basically strangle myself. Thankfully people were there each time and were able to save me.

Looking back, now I realize how close I came multiple times to dying. God wanted me to be here.

"Today is a beautiful day ---- because we woke up" —Keith Pate

"Sports are tough. Life is tougher. Never Quit!"

4

"TODAY IS A BEAUTIFUL DAY, BECAUSE WE WOKE UP"

Before my stroke, I took life and many things in it for granted. I had to think of things I'd never considered before, including the width of a door and whether it opened out, or if the floor was slick. I was telling my neighbors a few days ago that before I put a long-sleeve dress shirt on, I have to button the sleeves; otherwise, I'd never get them buttoned. Just an example of how differently I have to look at things now. Life is precious, and I no longer take days for granted as I once did.

Many friends and family members ask often how I tell crowds my story because they know I'm not a speaker. "I'm a back-row Baptist," I tell them. I feel I have an obligation as a Christian to tell others about the goodness of Christ and what he has done for me. We had a sermon at church on Christmas Eve 2018 about letting our light shine. I want to be a light for Christ. I often talk about perspective and how I've struggled with it. I've had to change my perspective often since my injury. I'm divorced and live alone. I was preparing for a speaking event and was ironing my clothes. I'm a military guy and got angry at myself because I was running late. I had to take a step back and remind myself to be thankful I could even iron.

Each person has a choice when listening to my story. It can be the saddest story you ever heard, or you can be awed at the power of the God we serve and be thankful of the fact that I survived. Know if he did it for me, he can do it for you.

I remind audiences I'm not a public speaker, I'm not a pastor or evangelist, and I don't do this for money. I'm just a normal guy with a story I need to tell, and you need to hear. I'm no different from any of you. I majored in beer drinking and chasing women in college, I've lied, and I've stolen. It's a good thing Jesus paid the price for anything and everything I've done.

I remember waking up in the hospital and being freezing. My temperature was so high the nurses and doctors had placed ice packs under my arms and between my legs to keep my temperature down, but I woke up.

You see, I'm not a believer because my mom took me to church every Sunday or because I read my Bible daily. These things are very important.

God has worked miracles in my life. I wouldn't be here today if he hadn't.

According to the Gospels, when Jesus entered Capernaum, the people heard that he had come home. They gathered in such large numbers that there was no room left, not even outside the door, and he preached the word to them. Some men came, bringing to him a paralyzed man, carried by four other people. Since they could not get him to Jesus because of the crowd, they made an opening in the roof above Jesus by digging through it and then lowered the mat the man was lying on. When Jesus saw their faith, he said to the paralyzed man, "Son, your sins are forgiven."
—Mark 2:1-5 (NIV)

5

HEALING THE PARALYTIC

It's not difficult to find stories of overcoming struggles in the Bible. I was discussing my story with a friend and we found no better example than this. The paralytic man symbolizes me, and the large crowd symbolizes the struggles I would encounter and must overcome. All my help (medical professionals, family, friends, neighbors, etc.) took me to the roof and lowered me, allowing me to reach help. I must say I've found nothing to replace hard work. A work ethic is a gift from God. So many times, I wasn't able to rely on intelligence. I was able to rely on my work ethic. Thanks to God and my help, I'm on my way to being the best I can be.

6

SPORTS

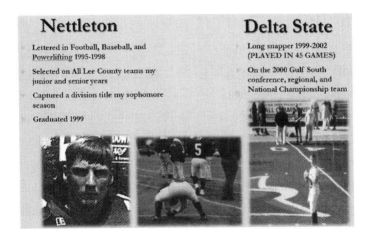

Nettleton

Lettered in Football, Baseball, and Powerlifting 1995-1998

Selected on All Lee County teams my junior and senior years

Captured a division title my sophomore season

Graduated 1999

Delta State

Long snapper 1999-2002 (PLAYED IN 45 GAMES)

On the 2000 Gulf South conference, regional, and National Championship team

Sports have always been a huge part of my life. I'm very passionate about athletes using their platform to reach others and about teaching them that sports are hard but life is much harder. I was coming to the end of my football career at Delta State University. I had been on several teams in the past, but what was I to do now? Most of my life, I had poured my heart and soul into sports. I don't believe

I made bad decisions with life, but things would've been much easier if I'd had the relationship with Christ I needed.

I was an all-county offensive guard in high school. I had no idea I could play college ball anywhere. I was joining the military right out of high school. When Delta State called and asked me to try out, I put my recruiter and military paperwork on hold. About twenty snappers showed up on tryout day, and I was stunned when I was selected to play for the Statesmen. I told my recruiter I'd be back in four years. And I was.

Long snappers are specialists like kickers and are often thrown into the same category. We were good and performed well when called on. We practiced separate from the team most times. I remember showing up to my first practice. We had three great snappers on the team. The rest of the snappers brought balls to practice with; I snuck a twenty-five-pound weight out. I would snap that weight across the practice field and back. I thought it couldn't hurt. I eventually won the starting job. (Desperate times call for desperate measures.)

Most players wanted my job until game time and all eyes were on you. I learned early that muscle memory was the best way for me to deal with pressure. I promise when you're punting from your end zone or kicking a game-winning field goal, you'll need a way to deal with pressure. I used it often. I still use those techniques today. You didn't want people to know your name, you didn't want to be in the papers, and you definitely didn't want to be on the highlight video. (Usually this was for bad reasons.) We had it easy, right? But thankfully God had blessed me and the rest of my squad with a great work ethic. The coaches also included us in everything. I noticed early in my career that our hard work was paying off with other players and coaches. We ran every sprint and did every workout.

I remember our strength and conditioning coach created a goal for winter workouts called an "Iron Statesmen." Every player, including me, wanted to be one. We had several events that we were measured in, and we had to achieve a certain predetermined goal in each event to be titled an "Iron Statesmen." I was going to do everything I could to earn that title. But how realistic was it that the long snapper reached this goal? I remember anxiously waiting for the names to be published. I was beyond ecstatic when I saw my name. I still have the shirt from the photo we took, but that's a title I'll never forget, and that earned me lots more respect among the players. I went from being a long snapper to a teammate and brother who was the long snapper.

Early in my sporting career, I experienced the difference in really good teams and really bad teams. I was honored to be on the 2000 national championship team while at DSU. I was on four different teams at Delta State. Honestly, I was part of more talented teams than the 2000 team. It wasn't until later in life that I really wondered why we were so good. That 2000 team was the most unselfish team I had ever been a part of. We played for each other, not worrying about stats and numbers. Those came, but we didn't want to let each other down. As a military leader later and a father now, I try to teach others the same values.

I recall it being early December 2000 and we had just won the national championship. My head was so big I wonder how it fit in my car to travel home. I thought I was someone important. People wanted my autograph!

I worked those holidays to buy gifts. I had just gotten off work on December 26, 2000. I was visiting with a coworker. My phone rang, and someone told me they needed me to come to the hospital. My mom had been placed there. My friend drove me. I remember so many things going through my mind. When I arrived, my mom was in septic shock and her organs were shutting down. She was twice her normal size. She had tubes and wires running from every orifice in her body. She had been beaten, so she was now fighting for her life. Why? I had just helped win the championship a couple of weeks before. How could my life change so drastically and so suddenly? It was like being hit in the stomach with a baseball bat by Babe Ruth. It was the most helpless I'd ever felt.

A few days later, the doctor called my brother and me in the hall. I was nineteen and he was eighteen, and we decided to pull the plug on our mother. On December 29, 2000, my mother took her last breath at thirty-six years of age. One year younger than I am now. Her assaulter was now a murderer.

My family and the prosecution would ensure he paid. The trial was harder than the hospital because I had to relive those events through captured photos and testimonies. Her killer was sitting just feet from us. Before the verdict was read, I remember standing up and speaking for the family. I told the court that I wished I had beautiful mental pictures to remember my mom by, but the memories I would have of her forever were the ones of her double her normal size with tubes and wires coming from her body. Those images were branded in my mind.

The day we had her funeral, many of the 2000 team, including the head coach, were there. I remember being very surprised when they walked in. We had just won the championship and were on the highest athletic level as a team. As a person, I was at my lowest at that time. They probably didn't know the impact of their actions. I would never forget them being there and supporting me. I've learned so much about unselfishness from them.

I gave my mom such a hard time growing up. We were so similar that we often butted heads. My son and I are the same way now. Looking back, I wish I hadn't been so difficult. She was very creative and could do anything. She was searching for love, and that eventually killed her. She just wanted to be loved. She would paint yard signs and ornaments for Christmas or Halloween, make and decorate cakes for birthdays or weddings, and sew dresses for Easter. She could write calligraphy or build a house if she needed. I'll probably lose my man card for admitting it, but I remember helping her do many of those things. I got her cake-baking supplies after she passed. She was a servant; she loved to make people happy. I always wondered where I got my creativity and my willingness to try to succeed at anything. We were never rich growing up, but our parents ensured we had what we needed. She was so excited when we went from a single-wide trailer to a double-wide. You would've thought we had a mansion. My biggest wish is that she would've met her grandkids. I know she would've loved my two as much as I do. She would enjoy doing some of her crafts with them. She would see herself in them like I do.

"I enjoyed the teamwork and family aspect of football so much that when it was over I joined the military so I could continue to be part of a team." -Keith Pate

7

MILITARY

I hung up my football cleats and laced up combat boots just after graduating college in 2003. Obviously I was no smarter after college than before. I'd heard many stories growing up from my grandpa (William Dallas Pate). He had served in the army during World War II. I remember winning an essay contest when I wrote about him while I was in high school. He'd never told me bad stories, and I wanted to be just like him. I wanted to serve my country. I called my recruiter just before I graduated college, just as I had told him I would. There was something patriotic in my blood.

I enlisted as a combat medic in the Mississippi Army National Guard in the 1-198 Armor Battalion, 155 Heavy Brigade Combat Team in Amory, Mississippi, in 2003. I remember wondering what I had gotten myself into while in basic training. I had just turned twenty-two and was considered one of the old men in my platoon. Most guys were eighteen or nineteen years old. It was amazing to me that some guys had never fired a gun. I was from the south. It was a rite of passage for me. I assumed it was for everyone. While at training, I fell in love with the military. It was a perfect fit, and I was good at being a soldier. I went to San Antonio, Texas, after basic training for my medical training. In college, I had studied computers, so I still wonder why I became a medic. After my initial training, I learned my unit had been alerted to deploy. I was assigned as a medic for our scout platoon.

Each state has a small support system of active guard reserve soldiers (AGR) who are full time and hired to support the traditional guard. I was informed of an opening, but I found out recruits had to go through a strict board process to be hired. Then they were treated just like an active duty soldier, but they had the option to live within the community. All I knew was I wanted to be one. I studied and was selected for the job. I was the only soldier to apply, so it wasn't a difficult choice. No one else wanted to go to Iraq. I was already going. I went to El Paso, Texas, for training. My supervisor then was Staff Sergeant Michael Hollings. He and I became extremely close throughout my career.

As part of our train up for OIF 3, we did about 180 days of training at Camp Shelby Training Center and about a month at the National Training Center (NTC) in Fort Irwin,

California, before deployment. I have memories of horrible meals ready to eat, full Porta-Johns, winter, cold showers, night shift, and no cell phone service. (Important to me at the time.) My daughter was born while I was in California. She is now much older and doesn't remember those times, but I do. You don't understand those guys' sacrifice until you've been there and done that. I would climb nearby mountains (with my partner in crime, Jesse Lindsey) late at night and make homemade antennas to get cell service to call home. It was absolutely killing me not to be there. We spent Thanksgiving (the meal could have been worse) at the NTC, but most were able to go home for Christmas before deploying to Iraq.

We were stationed on a small base just outside An Najaf. An Najaf is located just south of Baghdad. It is also considered the southern tip of the triangle of death. We did about a ten-month tour. I was awarded the Meritorious Service Medal for my service there. Throughout the brigade, we would lose twenty-eight souls during this mobilization. It's been fifteen years since the mobilization, but their sacrifice seems like yesterday. I find myself speechless when writing about them. I'll forever be grateful!

After returning home, Michael was promoted and was replaced by then Sergeant First Class Donald Spikes. He served as my supervisor for about one year before moving and taking a different job. During this time, our battalion reorganized as the 1-98 Cavalry Squadron. His vacancy left an opening and an opportunity for me. I interviewed and was accepted as the battalion/squadron senior human resources NCO (sink or swim). I inherited a huge responsibility. I had great supervisors before, and I was ready. (I hoped.) I was responsible for the human resources for about a thousand soldiers spread over eight locations. I was forced to develop my organizational skills. To help me, we built a dream team consisting of then Staff Sergeant Samuel Gilleylen and then Sergeant Christopher Coker. Chris would fight a valiant battle against sarcoma and ultimately loose his battle. He was part of my team, and I definitely wouldn't be successful without him. He is deeply loved and missed. He is greatly respected by his peers and leadership. Those guys made my job easy, and I always felt that if I was going to drown, they would drown with me. I couldn't ask for better guys to work with.

In 2007, I was in decent physical shape and asked to attend some hand-to-hand combat training in Marana, Arizona, just outside of Tucson. Maybe my leadership knew I was dumb enough to go. Modern combatives, level 1. They would teach us mostly ground fighting, which is very similar to what you see in the Ultimate Fighting Competition (UFC). But moves you could do with body armor on. We were also trained to fight for our life. There were about fifteen soldiers in the class. At the end of each day, we were told to form two large circles. One inner circle and one outer circle, and each person was facing another. We would fight that person on our knees until the whistle blew and the inner circle would rotate one space to the right. We would do that until everyone fought. That was our conditioning for the day. I came back with badly stained and torn uniforms, but I graduated and was able to train soldiers within our brigade on what I learned. I knew just enough to get beat up.

My very close friend and partner in crime, then Staff Sergeant Jesse Lindsey, would train for and win the soldier of the year competition in 2007. He won the state, region, and the First Army competitions. One of my greatest accomplishments was meeting him early mornings for a road march or a run to prepare for his competitions. I also trained him in combatives. I didn't have the time to teach him everything, so I made him an expert in one move. That move would be successful in most occasions. I helped him any way I could. Jesse would eventually become a warrant officer, and I would become an officer. He and I would take our oaths on the same day in a joint ceremony. You have those you consider friends, and then you have those you consider brothers. He and Michael are brothers.

About a year after taking that job in Amory, we could see another mobilization coming quickly. My wife and I discussed seriously the best options for me to take for the future and for my family. I already had a college degree and had actually begun working toward my master's degree. They were about to start the next Officer Candidate School (OCS) class so I decided to join the accelerated class that lasted eight weeks. I delayed my commission after returning until I could find a full-time opportunity. In February 2008, I accepted my commission and was soon sent to my Basic Officer Leadership Course, phase 2, at Fort Benning, Georgia. I would then go to the Armor Basic Officer Leadership Course, phase 3, at Fort Knox, Kentucky. I got to go home on the weekends and spent several weeks between each phase at home. My wife was about to give birth to my son while I was in Kentucky, so we planned to induce labor on May 27, 2008. I was able to be there for his birth, but I had to return for a couple of weeks of training before graduating.

I graduated Basic Officer Leadership Course (BOLC), phase 2, as an honor graduate in February 2008. And I graduated on the Commandants' List in Armor BOLC 3. (Good thing they didn't just look at intelligence in those courses.) In July 2008, I was interviewed and hired as the full-time squadron training officer. It was rare that a new lieutenant was hired here, but I'd had several years of experience enlisted and again I was ready. (I hoped again.) This was a captain's slot, but I couldn't be promoted until I reached my time in grade as a lieutenant.

I would be activated as a platoon leader for Hurricane Gustav in August later that summer. This would be my first role as a new officer. I had a very experienced platoon sergeant and realized my platoon would respect me more because of the time that I spent as enlisted. They worked extremely hard for me. Something amazing about spending a tremendous amount of time preparing then giving soldiers a mission and working with them and seeing them work so hard to accomplish that mission. My platoon and I sat on the beach in our Humvees, watching the hurricane approach over the water. It was frightening but amazing to watch. Our platoon supported half of Gulfport, the second largest city in Mississippi. We conducted over 250 door-knock missions and distributed two semitruck loads of ice and water.

During my career, I would get so caught up in the politics of the military, but I tried never to forget the simple *why* I did what I did.

In May 2009, we were activated to deploy to Iraq for the second time, this time for OIF 9.2. We would only do a forty-five-day train up at Camp Shelby before leaving. This time, things would be much different for me. I'd be deploying as an officer and my squadron commander wanted me to take the role of the support operations officer during the deployment. We were at a base just outside of Tikrit. This would be a huge job with a huge responsibility. I would be replacing Major Bender from a unit in California. I would learn that every mission we would run would cross my desk. We performed convoy security and worked hand in hand with a transportation unit on our base. I would do all the coordination with that unit and ours for each mission. I was going to be the best SPO I could. I'd been a part of this unit for about six years and knew most of the soldiers personally. I was in a position to affect their lives and took it personally. Sometimes I took things too personally. I was awarded the Bronze Star Medal for my service there. In March 2010, our deployment would be over, but stressful times and real-life struggles would continue.

I requested to transfer to a sister battalion, the 2-198 Combined Arms Battalion, located in Senatobia, Mississippi, to be close to my children, who had recently moved. I was the logistics officer for one of the largest battalions in the state. Once again, this was a captain's slot, but I couldn't be promoted until I reached my time in grade as a lieutenant. I reached my time in grade while in the hospital. I was promoted and pinned at a ceremony in Amory while on a rolling walker. I remember being very surprised at who all attended. You never realize the lives and careers you've impacted, but I hope they know how much they all impacted mine.

The battalion was a monster that stretched over eleven different locations. I would need experience in this area if I was going to continue my career. In June, I was transferred there. I was responsible for more than $150 million of battalion equipment. I had a very experienced and trained logistics staff. I would soak up all the information I could. Honestly, I didn't think about how much I was responsible for or how large we were. This was quite different from my previous duties in human resources and training. The logistics staff, being very experienced and knowledgeable in logistics, would drag my very newly learned skills through a six-battalion new equipment fielding.

I was and still am a big proponent of health. I was able to

acquire gym equipment and combative equipment for seven of our locations. I helped train a couple of soldiers in hand-to-hand combatives to help prepare them for an upcoming soldier of the year competition.

I was just learning to spell logistics when I would have my stroke in December 2010. Then I would return to serve a short time in 2012 until my medical packet was finished and I was medically retired on December 27, 2012. I was medically retired as an armor-qualified captain with over nine years of service and two deployments to Iraq as a member of the 2-198 Combined Arms Battalion, 155 Brigade Combat Team.

I learned so much and served with so many great people I still consider great friends. Those people helped mold and fine-tune me into the person I am now. The difficult circumstances we went through together would help prepare me for what I would face. I have received many awards and served in many different areas. But the people I served with and the memories we shared were my real awards. I used Jesse to help me recall some memories. He said, "The military teaches us to do our best in the hardest of times." As you can see from my story, I can't agree any more.

Since my retirement, I have had issues with seeing people in uniform or visiting some of our units and being reminded of such a large part of my life. I'm slowly learning to deal with it, but it's a struggle.

- Enlisted as a Medic, Later become an Officer
- Medically Retired as a Captain (O3-E)
- Member of the Active Guard Reserves(AGR) for the Mississippi Army National Guard
- 9 years of service
- 2 Iraq Deployments, 2004(Najaf) & 2009(Tikrit)
- Squadron Support Operations Officer (SPO) during 2nd deployment
- Bronze Star Recipient

Being different
Stares
People feeling sorry for me
Slower than most causing impatience
People saying I can't

8

CHALLENGES

These are a few of the challenges I have to deal with. I'm different. I'm that weirdo. My kids have that guy as a father. I'm used to the stares now, but they affect anyone I'm with also. If you could see me, I walk with a crutch, and that draws a lot of attention most places I go. I enjoy rock-wall climbing, but on first impression, most people would say I can't. I love when people say I can't. Those thoughts are free motivation to prove people wrong. I love challenges.

THE HEART OF A CHAMPION NEVER QUITS

- With the help of many others I had to learn to do everything again
- (Walk, Write, Tie shoes, Everything)
- Progress was hard but it came.

9

THE COMEBACK

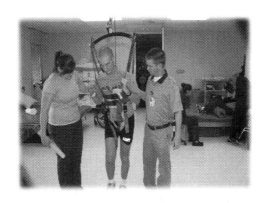

After my stroke, I had to learn to do everything again. My neighbor said he had never seen such a determined look in my eyes. Imagine having your master's degree and learning to write your name again. That's my wheelchair in the background, and thankfully it's now sitting in a garage with two flat tires and dust all over it. It's for sale, if anyone would like it. I included this other picture to show my progress but also to show that we had a lot of support throughout my stay there. I remember learning to brush my teeth again. My coordination was so bad that I couldn't go up and down. I had to insert my toothbrush end into a tennis ball and hold the ball as I brushed. It must have worked because my dentist never complained and my teeth didn't fall out.

10

GOOD EXAMPLE

The Power of a Good Example

I can't throw a football or command a tank any longer, but these are events I've found I can do. On first impression, most people would say I can't. I've fallen in love with these events, and I've found them to provide me with a challenge. It hasn't been my goal, but I'm very thankful that I can be an inspiration to most. If they see me doing these events, they'll probably ask, "Why can't I?"

I like a challenge. You're not going to see me sitting

much. I started climbing on a wall at the hospital in Augusta, Georgia, with an adaptive coach. I've kept up climbing even after returning home. The Wounded Warrior Project has been wonderful and provided a life coach to help me with these events.

In late July, I was invited to go on a Soldier Ride in New York City. The Memphis VA has been great and helped me get a recumbent bike. I've always ridden my bike, but I wasn't inspired to do it seriously until the ride. On the Soldier Ride, we rode approximately seventy miles in three days. After returning home, I was still inspired, and the first week of September, I rode 131 miles in a week. According to most auto insurance computers, the average car travels sixteen miles per day, which means 112 miles per week. On October 13, 2018, I rode 37.9 miles in one day. I don't state these things to brag but to issue a challenge to people. It doesn't have to be riding a bike, but be an inspiration to others. I promise someone is watching.

11

COULD BE WORSE

I've been blessed throughout my injury (even though my situation is horrible), and even now, I'm reminded of how things could be worse.

I was in the hospital with a former Navy Officer, Brad Snyder; he's 100 percent blind. (https://youtu.be/ uQVg6Fvu5ZM) He is still an inspiration to me. He'll never be able to see his kids or wife. In the 2016 Paralympics Games in Rio, he won three gold medals and one silver medal in swimming. They put a tennis ball on the end of a blind pole and tap him on the head when it's time to turn.

I rode in the Soldier Ride with a group of amputee veterans from the United Kingdom. They are all inspirations, but one guy is a triple amputee who only has one good right arm. I watched him and others ride seventy miles on a hand bike. When I felt tired and wanted to quit, there was no excuse that I could use to compete with their situations. I had to keep going.

Don't feel sorry for me or yourself.

12

TEAM PATE

My New Team

Although I'm no longer at DSU or in the military, I'm still on an important team. I'm like my kids' quarterback. We have an awesome head coach in God. It goes back to doing the things I can now. I know they're watching. I can't teach them to throw a ball, but there are much more important lessons I can teach them. Life will throw you curveballs, and

Satan will want you to give up. They know Dad never gives up and he gets his strength from our God.

I'm very proud of my children and the people they're growing to be. They've both been lifesavers for me in more than one way. I like to go to every event of theirs I can. I don't go to coach, although I do get caught in the moment some. I missed so much of their childhood unwillingly. I spent so much time on deployments, in schools, and then in the hospital. (They might try to trade me in.) I find it amazing watching them run and participate in activities. Knowing something I influenced can independently do those things. *Crazy.*

Both are great athletes, very hardworking, and great academically. My daughter has three national championship rings in competitive cheerleading. She can tumble so well. She likes to scare me to death on the trampoline. Her school is known as the best of the best in cheerleading, but I've seen how hard they work and how much they practice while maintaining their academics.

My son is an awesome competitive baseball player. He's ten years old and can hit from both sides of the plate. He has amazing hand-eye coordination. I tell him often, "If I would've had a quarter of the talent you have, I would've been trouble." He just started playing ice hockey and I'm amazed at how fast he's picked up on the game.

They both understand that their relationship with God and their academics are most important. Their platform as an athlete can be used to benefit God.

13

HELP OF OTHERS

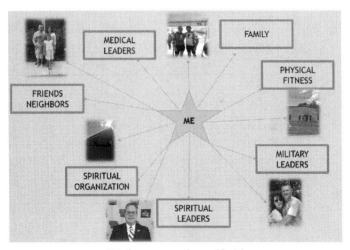

Tried to surround myself with
Help and Encouragement

My kids are very important team members, but they aren't the only members. God has blessed me by putting some amazing people in my life. I can't begin to explain the importance of having a great support system in place. From medical experts to friends that I can rely on, all are very important. I've realized they are watching me too, and if they see me giving my best, they are going to give me their best.

Yes, I'm even a member at a gym. You can only imagine some of the looks I get when I jump on a treadmill beside someone. They usually speed up and stay on until I get off.

I am an American Soldier.
I am a warrior and a
member of a team.
I serve the people of the United
States, and live the Army Values.
I will always place the mission first.
I will never accept defeat.
I will never quit.
I will never leave a fallen comrade.
I am disciplined, physically and
mentally tough, trained and proficient
in my warrior tasks and drills.
I always maintain my arms,
my equipment and myself.
I am an expert and I am a professional.
I stand ready to deploy, engage, and
destroy, the enemies of the United
States of America in close combat.
I am a guardian of freedom and
the American way of life.
I am an American Soldier.

14

SOLDIER'S CREED

I memorized the creed in my initial training. I still have it memorized and say it to myself daily, but I had never really listened to the words. If someone were to ask who Keith Pate is, I would refer them to this paragraph. The words are who I am. They are branded in me. This is the way I've tried to live my life, and I still try today.

BE A SOLDIER FOR CHRIST

ENLIST
>   SURRENDER YOUR LIFE TO JESUS
>   FIND A LOCAL BIBLE BELIEVING CHURCH AND JOIN THE FAMILY

TRAIN
>   GROW YOUR FAITH BY READING AND STUDYING GOD'S WORD
>   BE ACCOUNTABLE TO OTHER CHRISTIANS
>   ENJOY AN INTIMATE RELATIONSHIP WITH GOD THROUGH JESUS

DEPLOY
>   GO TELL OTHERS ALL THAT GOD HAS DONE FOR YOU AND INVITE THEM TO JOIN IN HIS WORK WITH YOU

15

SOLDIER FOR CHRIST

I realize not everyone (for whatever reason) can be an American soldier, but we all can be soldiers for Christ. I relate the three simple steps to each other. The same steps I used to be an American soldier would allow me to become a soldier of Christ. I invite you to deploy with me and become a soldier for Christ. Life has been guaranteed to be tough. You want to ensure you're on the right team *today*. Tomorrow is not promised. Take it from me.

Plan of Salvation

SALVATION NEEDED
Fact of Sin
>Romans 3:10; 3:23

Consequences of Sin
>Isaiah 59:2; Romans 6:23

SALVATION PROVIDED
John 3:16

SALVATION ACCEPTED
Repentance Required
>Acts 20:20, 21

Faith is Necessary
>Acts 20:20, 21

CLOSING VERSES
>Rev. 3:20; Romans 10:9 -13
>Romans 6:23; John 1:12

Confession - Mt. 10:32, 33

Baptism - Mt. 28:18 - 20

Church Membership -
>Mt. 28:18-20; Acts 2:41, 47

ACKNOWLEDGMENTS

I would like to thank God first and foremost. I would've never imagined that he would use my testimony as he has. I would like to give him all the glory. This is the story of how he has impacted my life.

I would like to thank all my military friends, leaders, teammates, coaches, and especially family members, without whose help this book would never have been completed. I didn't list many names because my life and career have been drastically impacted by so many. I know if I listed everyone, I'd leave someone out. Thanks to everyone.

Thank you for your patience and guidance. Thank you to all who have served and those who still serve.

If you want to experience the full impact of this book, I encourage you to put a face to the story. Invite me for a question-and-answer session or a meet and greet. Email me at <u>keithpate81@yahoo.com</u>.

WHAT OTHERS SAY

I consider myself very fortunate to have met Keith Pate. Before even knowing his story, I was already so impressed with his passion, dedication, and commitment to furthering God's kingdom through his work with the FCA. Then I got to hear him speak one day and saw true courage and grace up there behind that podium. As I learned more about his background, I am in awe of how God can use anyone in any circumstance to serve his purpose, and Keith has faithfully allowed him to do so in his own life. We serve an awesome God, and Keith is a living example of someone who is honoring him through the platform he has been given.

—Former New England Patriot and
Super Bowl champion David Nugent

Keith's story is motivational, uplifting, and inspirational at many levels. As a championship level collegiate athlete and a true warrior in the armed forces, Keith possesses all of the physical attributes and mental toughness that we typically think it takes to be successful, but his incredible story does a remarkable job of explaining to us that only a relationship and trust in God will deliver us into true contentment.

Keith's story is one of great highs, great valleys, and finally overcoming adversity.

—Former Delta State University and Current
South Alabama Head Coach Steven Campbell

At twenty-nine years of age, Keith was in his usual state of good health. However, on December 26, 2010, his life abruptly changed when he awoke with disequilibrium. Realizing that something very significant was amiss, he was transported to a local emergency room in Tupelo, Mississippi. Keith was ultimately diagnosed with cardioembolic cerebellar strokes due to an atrial septal defect. In brief, an atrial septal defect is a small hole in the heart that allows clots to travel from the venous to the arterial side of the circulatory system. Keith's hospital course was prolonged. He required a neurosurgical procedure, commonly known as a decompressive suboccipital craniectomy, to prevent sudden death due to cerebral edema (i.e., brain swelling). He also experienced multiple cardiopulmonary arrests. He had no clear-cut evidence for a hypercoagulable state (i.e., clotting disorder) and no previous history of strokes or stroke-like events. Due to increased intracranial pressure, Keith required continuous drainage of cerebrospinal fluid from the ventricles of his brain through a ventriculostomy tube. Magnetic resonance imaging of the brain showed that strokes had damaged almost the entirety of his cerebellum. Ultimately, after clinical stabilization, he underwent extensive rehabilitation at the Shepherd Center in Atlanta.

Over many years, Keith consistently and aggressively worked on improving his overall neurological status and ambulatory abilities. His exercise routine included both aerobic and strength training. In addition, he received vestibular rehabilitation to improve his balance, gait, and eye movements. Overall, he has shown dramatic neurological improvement far beyond what could be expected for a man without a cerebellum.

The cerebellum is a complex, intricate, highly lobulated structure at the back of the brain that plays a critical role in all voluntary movements, including writing, eating, walking, and talking. The cerebellum receives information from the spinal cord, vestibular apparatus in the inner ear, and other parts of the brain to regulate motor activity. The cerebellum is particularly important for precise movements that depend on accurately coordinated timing of muscle contractions. Without a cerebellum, patients may exhibit a tremor when reaching for objects and have difficulty walking and speaking. In some patients, other portions of the brain may compensate, in part, for loss of normal cerebellar functioning.

—*Mark S. LeDoux, MD, PhD/director,*
Movement Disorders, Wesley Neurology Clinic,
and professor, University of Memphis

Captain Keith Pate served under my command in the 155th Armored Brigade Combat Team. Keith is one of the best soldiers who I have served with in my thirty-five years of military service. Keith is a combat-proven officer with natural leadership qualities and soldier skills. He exemplifies the warrior spirit in every measurable means. He accomplished all assigned task at a high degree of success. He was a fitness junky who consistently earned the Physical Fitness Badge on the Army's Physical Fitness Test (APFT). He ran half marathons, practiced martial arts, and utilized CrossFit as part of his workout. His endurance, hardworking habits, and devotion to duty in both combat and training environments were relentless. Keith's potential in the Mississippi Army National Guard was unlimited. He was being groomed to assume duties and responsibilities at the higher ranks. He was a future commander and senior staff officer. Even though Keith's military reputation preceded him, he was a humble servant who never took credit for his work or achievements. He was the ultimate team player who was highly admired and respected by his peers, subordinates, and superiors alike.

I was in Memphis with my daughter scheduled to have her tonsils removed when I received word that Keith's condition had gotten worse. He was scheduled for emergency surgery with not much hope of surviving. I was in disbelief that this was happening to Keith. He had endured so much over the past ten years—tragic loss of his mother and two combat deployments to Iraq—and now his life hung in the balance and also the outlook for his two young children. Even if he survived, he had a long and grueling rehab ahead with limited recovery.

In March 2011, I visited with Keith in Atlanta. I was touched to see him. We communicated with each other the best we could. Based on Keith's character, we knew he'd surpass the expectations held by the medical professionals. Upon Keith's return to Mississippi in 2012, we promoted him to captain on December 24 and presented him an award for his devoted service to the Mississippi Army National Guard. Keith was wearing his dress blue uniform for the occasion. It was an honor for me to take part in the ceremony.

God's work moves in mysterious ways that our mortal minds do not understand. For reasons only known to God, the Almighty closed the chapter on Keith's remarkable military career and handpicked him to serve for the kingdom.

With the same devotion and passion, Keith "charlie mikes" (Army slang for continues mission).

In summary, I am blessed to know Keith Pate. His story is a reflection of who he is and what he represents. By no fault of his own, Keith's life took a different turn. Many would have given up on life and cursed God for their fate. Rather than praying for personal protection, a combat soldier often prays to accept the Lord's outcome. Keith accepted God's will and has remained faithful to our Savior's plan for his life.

—*John M. Rhodes, Brigadier General and former*
155 Brigade Combat Team Commander

Keith is such an unbelievably strong, Christian man providing a true a role model for all of us by his actions. I so remember how much I respected his intellect, strong work ethic, and passion for being a soldier and leader and still do to this day. I will never forget the day we first met when he was interviewing for the full-time training officer position with 1-98 CAV. I was blown away by his competence and confidence he showed during the interview. His passion for the soldier's well-being is the single most impression trait I respect about him.

—*John Nipp, Colonel and Former*
Commander of the 1-98 CAV

I've known Keith Pate as an NCO and having the distinct honor of pinning him as a lieutenant upon his commissioning as an officer. His inspiring journey that's detailed in his book, although remarkable, isn't unexpected from a person of his integrity, conviction, and more importantly, love of life. His book is a great, inspiring story of his journey and is a testimony for us all that, through his example of personal courage, faith in family, and friends, Christ conquers all things.

—*Darrell Bolin, president and CEO of operations, Americas, ThyssenKrupp Elevator, and former executive officer of 1-98 Cavalry Squadron*

It was post-9/11 and at the height of the invasion of the Iraqi War. All of the military services were getting their share of the wartime efforts, which created a surge in recruiting efforts. Anthony Pearson was our local recruiter back then, and I will never forget him telling me about the homerun he had hit with a guy from Nettleton. He told me that he had never had a recruit put him on hold for four years while they excelled as a collegiate student athlete, but Keith Pate had graduated from Delta State University and would be joining us soon after he finished his initial entry training. It wasn't too long afterward that I walked in his office and there stood Keith. I knew of him from being local and the social circles but didn't really "know" him. I remember sizing him up like young men do and thinking, *This guy is a beast!* He was handsome, a physique of perfection, extremely smart, and well-spoken. He was humble and eager to learn everything about the unit and organization that we were in. The leadership of the battalion immediately recognized how special he was, and he was immediately hired as a full-time member of the team.

All of my life, I have been taught, trained, coached, and mentored that we are presumably scored or ranked off a finite set of rules with the main idea to win. Serving alongside Keith, it was evident that he was the guy who would master every finite game he signed up for. There was more to it than that for him. Keith was always planning and maneuvering for the infinite game of life. His mind worked at strategic heights, his motivation was second to none, and he had a work ethic that would rival the Amish. Simply put, Keith looked at life through a different lens and could do anything, and anything he did, he was good at it.

We quickly jelled and developed a strong relationship. We worked together, trained together, and spent a great deal of personal time together. From every corner in Mississippi to Yellow Creek Waterfall at Pickwick Lake, the Mojave Desert, and the streets of Iraq, there wasn't much ground or water that we didn't cover. I have seen Keith excelling in all sorts of capacities. Whether it was shooting machine guns, double dating girls, water sports, four-wheeling, bar fighting, writing papers, or singing lullabies to his kids, he was good at everything.

I will never forget getting the call that night telling me that he was in the intensive care unit at Tupelo and that they thought that Keith had had a stroke. I made it there as quickly as I could and had a front row seat to what he was going through. I will never forget the neurosurgeon telling the entire family and friends that he had a very small chance of making it through the procedure. We all cried, prayed, and hoped that he would make it through it. I vividly remember the common theme that people were saying. "If anybody can make it, he will."

In my opinion, God did some of his best work putting Keith Pate on this earth, and he gave us all a blessing by delivering him through these unimaginable life experiences. As he has always done, he has taken these life experiences and is applying them forward. He has developed a platform that allows him to share his journey so that it can positively influence others. There are not many people in life who truly make others better, but Keith is one of them. God has always used Keith, and he continues to do so. I am forevermore grateful to have him as a friend and a brother in arms.

—*Jesse Lindsey, Chief Warrant Officer 4*

Once Keith was medically cleared, he was able to transfer to acute rehab, where I was able to work with him. As his occupational therapist, it was my role to help Keith become as independent as possible with his daily tasks so that he could return home. From the time we met, I knew Keith was a hard worker and that he had excellent family support and a strong faith that things were going to improve. I can honestly say that Keith Pate has been one of my favorite people that I've worked with in my career. Not only was his intrinsic motivation so clear, but anyone who spoke with him learned very quickly that he had so much to live for. And he didn't just want to live, but he wanted to thrive! He wanted to be able to not only care for himself but for his children. They were his primary motivators and were always at the front of his mind. Keith also has a tremendous support system—people who loved and prayed for him but also people visited him often and encouraged him in everything he was doing. In my time in this profession, I have seen many people who do not have others to support and encourage them, and unfortunately their results are not always as good as those who have a strong supportive system of advocates.

Keith also held strong to his faith throughout his healing process. He knew that God had a purpose for his life and that there was still a plan for him as he continued on this earth. Keith inspired me, and his faith built up my own faith! His desire to keep working, even when his body would refuse to do what he was attempting, was incredible. Heroic virtue and hope were demonstrated in his life daily. He exhibited a tremendous desire to overcome the physical obstacles that had been placed in front of him and embraced immense hope of what was to come! Keith has been an inspiration. He has continued his work since leaving rehab and is a beautiful example of faithfulness and perseverance. Not only has he been successful, but he is thriving! I believe that he has remained faithful to trusting in God's perfect plan for his life, and our God has remained faithful to Keith as well. His healing touch has been present in Keith's life in small and large ways and has allowed him to reach many people. Keith's testimony to God's faithfulness and God's healing power is miraculous! There has never been a question in my mind that God had *big* plans for Keith Pate, and I rejoice at the fact that Keith is living proof that we can do all things through Christ, who gives us strength.

—*Mary, occupational therapist*

I had the privilege of getting to know Captain Pate during his rehabilitation process at the Charlie Norwood VA in Augusta, Georgia. Following his stroke, he experienced changes to his mobility, use of his hands, and voice. He spent a total of eleven months participating in intensive physical, occupational, and speech therapy to improve his independence and communication abilities. In speech therapy, we spent many hours working on voice control to make it easier for him to talk with others. These therapy sessions allowed me the opportunity to know Captain Pate on a personal level as we would often discuss his children, career, and goals while completing voice exercises. His faith, love for his family, and love for his country were always undeniable. He maintained a positive attitude, joyful spirit, and sense of humor despite his challenges. He was well respected among the other soldiers as his attitude, hard work, and faith truly set him apart. Despite his personal struggles, soldiers flocked to him as a source of encouragement and motivation during their own rehab. It is such a blessing to see the God is continuing to use his hardships to minister to others.

—*Shannon, speech therapist*

I met Captain Pate during his rehabilitations program immediately following his stroke. Although he experienced physical deterioration resulting from the stroke, his spirit remained strong. This spirit and the desire to return to his children sustained him. Even in this deteriorated physical state, Captain Pate rallied the support of the troops and quickly demonstrated his leadership with the other active duty service members at the rehab unit. In my therapy area, we used activities that helped develop the visual abilities and perceptions as a child developed; therefore, many of these activities may appear as childlike games. Where many service members may question, Captain Pate jumped in wholeheartedly. Our weekly gang of Qwirkle developed into a camaraderie of healing bodies, minds, and spirits. Captain Pate's mind was quick, and he would always take the lead, but his heart was kind. He would give way to another if he saw that someone else needed a win for the day. I also worked with Captain Pate on the rock wall. I clearly remember the day when, despite his physical conditions, he ascended the wall. He never gave up, even when he slipped and literally left skin in the game that day. This climb epitomized his drive. It leaves me no surprise as I watch him on social media continue his progress and improvements. I also understand when I see him give credit to a higher power because he would never take credit for his successes but always lifted others up. I can see that same person in the man who lifts up his maker in thanks, and he continues to inspire me as much today as the first day I met him.

—*Vision therapist*

Keith Pate moved in across the street from us a year after his stroke. We were excited to meet our new neighbor, but we had a very energetic poodle puppy that also wanted to meet our new neighbors. He ran across the street and enthusiastically greeted Keith's aunt and friend. We were quickly told this can never happen again. Keith's friend and aunt said he was fragile and could not handle a large dog jumping on him. It is hard to imagine now, but Keith could not walk down his driveway without a walker and help seven years ago.

We watched Keith persevere day after day and make what the doctors called impossible become reality! One doctor told Keith about four years ago that he would never get any better than he was right then. This prognosis was hard for Keith to hear, but he once again picked himself up and persevered to get even better and do more than any doctor could imagine. He progressed from a walker to crutches, to one crutch, and finally to no crutches in the house. This doctor had no idea who he was talking to!

Keith is the most determined person we have ever met. He continues to overcome obstacles every day and never stops amazing us. He has flipped over tractor tires and ridden a bicycle for twenty miles at a time, just to name a few of the astonishing accomplishments we have seen. He has become a family member to us, and we are so thankful God chose him to be our neighbor.

—Shane and Carrie Wigley, Neighbors

KEITH PATE

Keith is a member of the Wounded Warrior Project and a severe stroke survivor. He was born in Tupelo, MS then raised in Nettleton, MS. He played high school sports at Nettleton High where he received his diploma in 1999. He played college football at Delta State University, where he was on the Division II 2000 National Championship Team. He also received his bachelors of business administration in 2003 majoring in Computer Information Systems. He served in the Active Guard Reserve (AGR) military program for the state of Mississippi for 9 years. He served in multiple positions as an officer and enlisted. While serving two tours in Iraq he received a Bronze Star and other awards for his service. He received his Masters Degree in 2008 from Touro University International majoring in Information Technology. Keith lives in Hernando, MS. He has two children. He is featured in the May 2013 issue of Good Health magazine published by The American Heart Association and is on the January 2019 American Family Radio's Exploring Missions podcast series. He is a member of Hernando Baptist Church in Hernando, MS.

MILITARY AWARDS AND COMMENDATIONS
Bronze Star Medal – 1
Meritorious Service Medal – 2
Army Commendation Medal – 2
Army Achievement Medal – 3
Iraq Campaign Medal – 2
Army Good Conduct Medal
National Defense Service Medal
Noncommissioned Officer Professional Development Ribbon
Army Service Ribbon
Armed Forces Reserve Medal with M device

STATE AWARDS:
Mississippi Commendation Medal – 1
Mississippi Medal of efficiency
Mississippi War Medal – 2
Mississippi Emergency Service Medal